Out of Canaan

Out of Canaan

P O E M S

Mary Stewart Hammond

W·W·Norton & Company

New York   London

Printed in the United States of America
The text of this book is composed in 12/14 Bembo
with the display set in Trump Mediaeval Semi Bold Condensed
Composition and manufacturing by the
Haddon Craftsmen, Inc.
Book design by Margaret M. Wagner
First Edition.

Library of Congress Cataloging-in-Publication Data
Hammond, Mary Stewart.
Out of Canaan : poems / by Mary Stewart Hammond.
p. cm.
I. Title.
PS3558.A453O87 1991
811'.54—dc20   91-10242

ISBN 0-393-03050-4
W.W. Norton & Company, Inc., 500 Fifth Avenue, New York, N.Y. 10110
W.W. Norton & Company, Ltd., 10 Coptic Street, London WC1A 1PU
1 2 3 4 5 6 7 8 9 0

Among the many whose enthusiasm has been quite vital to me, I wish to single out Sara de Ford for the rigor of her training in the craft and the initial push; Stanley Plumly for intuiting just how much countervailing force against all things other I needed and never failing to apply it; William Matthews for his steady wisdom in matters great and small; and the late Howard Moss for validating the loan of their confidence.

But most especially, for Arthur

Acknowledgments

I would like to thank the MacDowell Colony where many of the poems in this book were begun or completed.

Grateful acknowledgment is also made to the following magazines in which poems in this collection have previously appeared:

American Poetry Review:
"Second Sight"

The American Voice:
"Silence" (published under the title "July")

The Atlantic:
"Saving Memory"

Boulevard:
"Praying for Separation"
"Triptych with Missing Madonna"
"Snowbound in a Summer House off the Coast of Massachusetts"

Field:
"Canaan"
"Positive Thinking"
"World Without End"

The Gettysburg Review:
"Suffrage"

The New Criterion:
"Ecumenical Movements on a Coffee Table" (published under the title "Found Poem on the Coffee Table")
"Heirlooms Lost"

The New England Review and Bread Loaf Quarterly:
"Hubris at White, Ga."
Winner, Narrative Poem Contest

The New Yorker:
  "Small Talk"
  "Communion"
  "Cosmetics"
  "Slow Dancing in the Living Room: Thanksgiving"
  "Making Breakfast"
  "Paying Respects"
  "Grandmother's Rug"

The Paris Review:
  "My Mother-in-Law Sailing"

The Yale Review:
  "Accepting the Body"

"Slow Dancing in the Living Room: Thanksgiving" was also reprinted in the anthology *Wedding Readings: Centuries of Writing and Rituals for Love and Marriage,* edited by Eleanor Munro, Viking Penguin.

Contents

II Exile

"Memory is the only real estate."

— Vladimir Nabokov

*"I was left the legacy of a pile of stovewood
split by a man in the mute chains of rage.
The land he loved as landscape
could not unchain him. There are many,
Gentile and Jew, it has not saved. Many hearts have burst
over these rocks, in the shacks
on the failure sides of these hills. Many guns
turned on brains already splitting
in silence. Where are those versions?
Written-across like nineteenth-century letters
or secrets penned in vinegar, invisible
till the page is held over flame."*

from "Living Memory" by Adrienne Rich

I

Canaan

Saving Memory

Summer nights we put pennies on the track.
Even the station was quiet enough for crickets.
Mountains surrounded us, middling high and purple.
No matter where we stood they protected us
with perspective. People call them gentle mountains
but you can die in there; they're thick
with creeper and laurel. Like voodoo,
I drew pictures with a sparkler. A curved line
arced across the night. Rooted in its slope,
one laurel tree big as the mountain holding it.

You can hear the train in the rails.
They're round, not flat, as you'd expect,
and slick. We'd walk the sound, one step, two,
slip, on purpose, in the ballast, hopscotch
and waltz on the ties, watching the big, round eye
enter the curve and grow like God out of the purple,
the tracks turning mean, molten silver blazing
dead at us. We'd hula. Tango. And the first
white plume would shoot up screaming long, lonely,
vain as Mamma shooing starlings from her latticed pies.
Sing Mickey Mouse, the second scream rising long, again,
up and up. Stick our right hip out, the third
wailing. Give it a hot-cha hot-cha wiggle, the fourth
surrounding us. Wrists to foreheads, bid each other fond
adieus, count three, turn our backs, and flash it a moon,
materializing, fantastic, run over with light,

the train shrieking to pieces, scared, meaning it,
short, short, short, short, pushing a noise
bigger than the valley. It sent us flying,
flattened, light as ideas, back on the platform,
the Y6B Mallet compound rolling through
southbound, steamborne, out of Roanoke.

It wasn't to make the train jump the track
but to hold the breath-edged piece of copper
grown hot with dying, thin with birth,
wiped smooth of origin and homilies.
To hold such power. As big as the eye
of the train, as big as the moon burning
like the sun. All the perspective curved,
curved and gone.

Canaan

1

And we grazed in the first ridges
behind the Piedmont, toward the uttermost
part of the South creek. Lo,

wood smoke weaves ribbons
through fall days and the sun
skitters on tin roofs

like fat in a skillet. Here,
even the serpent is reluctant, dozes
in the sparse warmth

at the foot of tree stumps. Blessed
were the least of our brethren
for they ate with the wrong fork,

chased gravy around thick plates
with Wonder bread, didn't know
the Sabbath from Shinola, therefore

were we holy. They shall move
their lips when they read this
and ignite the words with an index finger
>   >   >

run under the lines. If you know you can leave
in the middle of the night in the middle of the war
with a full tank of gas,

ye will never know them.

2

That the call may come forth like Jedidiah,
fear not. In those mountain hollows,
we grew eggs and beets, lifted up our eyes

for wild mushrooms. And King James
opened and closed on us, seven days,
with the ecstasy of pump organs.

So it is, cabbage roses flare
on cold slipcovers and Mamma's shotgun
pauses on its peg leg

back of the door. For when you went forth
on visitations, your male flock
drew to the manse, thirsty for salt,

scared Mamma like daughters. Thus
were sour mash jars lined up
at the edge of the yard for targets.

> > >

And the steeple inched three times its length
across the onion grass, pointing East
to home. And the shadow of death

danced on good days in the corncrib,
by sunset had crept under the fence,
reaching for the root cellar. Only

the fast dark saved us.

3

And on the sixth day so also
did you labor, upstairs
preparing sermons, far from babies

congregating before Mamma
for mashed bananas, turnips, the wrong
salvation, our mouths open like fish

hungry for the hook. There, in an oak
swivel chair, you rocked the Bible,
your feet crossed on the desk. Whence

>   >   >
you went on your knees by the cot,
pressing your forehead into your fists.
We watched through the keyhole.

Come Sundays, I was old enough
to sit in your lap, count seeds,
the lumps of coal, the signed cuffs

in the collection plate. After, I rose up
magnified as the angels, soared
over Galilee down to Mamma,

never touching the stairs, anointed
by the lot of their inheritance,
by the smell of your shirt.

I think Mamma was jealous your coin
tethered her, made her belly so swollen
her footsteps rattled china. She would

press the small of her back
when the sun fell in windowpanes
across Deuteronomy and the yellow pine floor

I didn't need, calling.

Having Words, or, Life in the Backyard

Because, in make-believe rules are absolute,
that's why. Or our whole world vanishes.

—TEXAS LIL

Such names we called each other, my brothers and I—
Devil Dal, Brat-Bull Bill, a.k.a. The Pope Pious.
and Eaton Hammond Eggs—but mine was official.
To my parents, to my face, I was Bonbon.
Texas Lil to you. It was the sausage curls
and chipmunk cheeks. The Botticelli angel,
the aunts and grannies sighed, sending
dresses with ruffles. Duhh widdle Bonbon
has duh widdle halo, the brothers jeered, stealing
my best Carter's Lollipop underpants
from the bottom drawer and selling them
to Bruce and Bow Hood across the alley for 35¢
and a peep at the pickled fetuses their father kept
in canning jars in the basement they
were always trying to get me down to look at.
It's not just the earth the weak inherit.
You got to saddle up and ride West with the bandits

to boot, but there you can hear knees knocking when
Lil walks in the saloon. It's she who gives the orders
tough, straight-up, from the side of her mouth
to Dead-Eye Dal, Chief Walking Bull, and Eaton Nothing.
She can outcuss any snake-in-the-grass varmint
in the territory, and her cheeks are painted on
so she can have them or not,
depending. No one diddles Lil.
They know what she's packing

9

in her beaded reticule. No hombre would even think
to get her down in the basement to
look at his pickled fetus.
The double-cross is certain death. Only
once in Black Rock, did the cowboys and the Indians
not shoot straight, play to Bird-Brain Bonbon, whine
like weenie rattlers on a hot day
in the High Sierras, how Lil's side always won.
Lil stayed home on the ranch to flip flapjacks
in her black fishnet stockings, and suffer vapors
on her fringed chaise longue, waiting for the nincompoops
to come back empty-handed. Worse.
They brought the outlaws home for dinner.
Lil fed them their jerky and molasses. Told them after
it was really mushrooms grown in poo. Didn't tell them
about the chopped-up rattlers' venom sacs.
Didn't need to. Only

Bonbon got out alive.

Silence

Our father
has warned us and warned us. In tinted photos
Mother smiles and is very beautiful.
Copper hair curls pink on her shoulders.
But she wasn't quite right, our father said.
He tried to help her. He tried
to make her better. He tried to make her
more to his liking. It was for her own
good. His word was gospel.
She slammed kitchen cabinet doors in disbelief,
said his word was killing her.
Red hair makes you do that.
She should have listened. She should have been
quiet.

And Daddy was right. The surgeon's knife,
to show us, peeled back the white meat to expose
our mother's ribs, scored her belly purple
to deliver the womb, the ovaries
clenched on either side, tremoring in the sudden
gash of light. They had to get rid of all
that female trouble. This hurt him more
than her. He promised. We tiptoed around,
my brothers and I. Tried not to cry.
It makes your milk come in. What
do they do with the trouble?
Maybe her insides wait in heaven.

They left one breast. It hangs like memory,
its red-eyed nipple gnawed, sucked large.

We drank her dry, she'd brag on us, drew
blood, sometimes. And she sang "Bye-Baby Bunting."
When she undresses, the nipple stares at us. It
stares and stares.
You have to look dead at it.
Or else. You get the picture. That vision
blinded with answers, that clean slate begging
for another chance, her dumb thigh grafted shiny
across her cage. It's enough to make your milk
come in. I bind my chest against her, the whole
lopped-off side, the milk-glass scar nuzzled
with light and the shadows of our heads.
We are on tiptoe backing away.
Her feet are gross and swollen.

Our mother was 33. The only girl, I am 11
going on 12. Survival hangs on slow calenders.
No wiggling or squirming. Please.
5-year anniversaries grow like pearls
around July. Not a peep! Our mother is better.
And 38. And 43. We celebrate in restaurants
hushed with linen cloths. And she is 48.
We are faint with briny candlelight.
She has oysters and saves the shells.

53. 58. We nurse her milestones
around our tongues like pagan
worry beads and bow our heads for blessing,
hope she'll be good, mumble her remaking,
grateful, truly, for this food

we are about to receive, these veal chops
braised in lemon marmalade, the potatoes dauphinois,
the pink champagne. Her hair looks tinted.
My brothers' towheads are dark as voices.
They are deacons they'll have you know.
I'm all arms and legs, always the bean pole.
It's always July. Listen
to the ticking. In inevitable hospitals you have
your choice: IV bottles or straws bent
in squat glasses of frosty water.
Criss Cross Applesauce. Her heart
is caught in my throat. But you won't catch me
crying. She had
fair warning.

Home Soil

I caught on to Korea, McCarthy, Vietnam
early. Different wars. One country. Divided
the way I was divided, made the Bull Run
and Manassas of domestic bliss. Either
I was "every bit Daddy" or "just like Mamma,"
nothing, if not dangerous. In countries where
everyone looks alike, the enemy is not discernible.
Even kids and grannies are known hand-grenade carriers.
That's why they have pockets in their pinafores. And
wear coolie hats. They run in circles, amoral, loyal.
Logic gets them coming and going. The very sight
can break your heart or knock you dead. Best
both sides should waste them, ambush them
leaning elbows on sunshine and leaf shadows
dappling kitchen counters, eating cinnamon toast,
watching the Hearings with colored Mamma May.
The day the lawyer, any grown-up, dared say,
"Sir, have you no decency?" tears shot out of me.
The old black woman held me in her arms,
crooning, secret with hymns, until dinner.

Old soldiers fade away in Florida citrus groves
on their 38th parallel, leaving their battleground
buckled with winter and land-mines, swollen with want.
Mamma could murder my Jesus Christ jaw-line,
Daddy-blue eyes, and yellow hair, all that smacks
of her mate, and Daddy dies to wring Mamma's mouth,

the too-effusive Methodist warmth, the lower lip
full of injury and dawdle, the way I tell tales
as if I had all day in an aluminum glider.
Christians, I'm your offering, dressed for the jungle
in pink bow-ribbons and pinafores, zigzagging
through the fire of your M-16s like an enemy guerrilla.
I should stand still and let you kill each other.
How many of us holding hands, swaying on the wind
in Alabama, boiled on the spray of fire hoses, singing
"We Shall Overcome" in Washington with daffodils
for bayonets, sure as shooting of the balm
in Gilead, were also crooning, secret with hymns,
for someone earlier than ourselves?

Positive Thinking

Mom have secret power to divine authentic
thought and feeling, precisely what wrong
with other people. And she always right.
This no humdrum ESP or witchy ordination.
Little bird knock on her sleep and tell her
truth. In latest poop she see

I malignant. Doctors look concern.
Doctors no understand Mom speak in metaphor.
She also dream. They sharpen scalpels.
I say "Mom, let's no tell anyone
what you think of me." She promise
she wouldn't, and she keep her promise,

she say. She only tell few aunts and uncles,
brothers, cousins, hairdressers, and every
prayer group from Richmond to Key West
her opinion. They all assume missionary
position, unbuckle my breasts, unscrew
my uterus, hold them up to God's radiation—

in Southeast U.S. is okay to parade children
naked without G-string for Jesus; it only give
goose bumps and metastasize doubt. Doctors
cut me open, search high and low for her faith.
Nothing. Not irreligious cell in my body.
Every hair benign. They stitch me up.

>   >   >

Greatest hospital on earth say
Mom wrong. I call to tell her. I say,
"Mom, you wrong. I have proof.
Pages and pages of proof. Many lab report.
I not malignant. I benign."
"That the power of prayer," she say.

Small Talk

Of course, a Belle should never seem
eager, but she could take longer
to get fixing to go than anyone
on God's green earth. Grandpop,

by his own reckoning, devoted 12/10ths
of his life to cooling his heels, but
after his funeral she didn't flirt.
She mounted the stairs, packed

her pocketbook with vitamins, Ex-Lax,
two pots of rouge, and a fresh
monogrammed hanky, soaped off her
engagement rings, hers and her mother's,

marking one for each granddaughter, took
off her clothes, pulled back the covers
and lay down next to the empty bed.
It would take six months, earth time.

It took so long, some days it turned her
mulish. She stopped eating to hurry up,
and shrank from her skin, though
the baby-fine hair it was whispered

she dyed, stayed chestnut. Her children
wheedled, wept, reasoned, put her

in a metal crib to keep her. She rattled
the bars; she took them for Jacob's ladder.

They hired nurses the size of Gabriel.
She hunkered down, waiting for herself,
not losing memory, as family would have it,
but forgetting what suited.

I tiptoed in from Maryland, wanting
to surprise her. "You didn't forget,"
she said. "Forget what?" I said.
"You promised you'd come back in time."

I sat on a stool between their beds, the way
I'd grown, in part, and held those
unengaged hands. T'weren't a thing wrong
with her she said; she was just dying.

And she stopped for a spell so we could visit.
For three days we went at our topics,
their litany putting us in fine fettle.
Her great-granddaughter lollygagged

on the foot of the bed. "Your daughter,"
she reminded us six times, "gets her coloring
from Pop, you know. But that figure
she got from me." Like congregation, glo-

>   >   >

rious, we'd sing the last line with her:
"She sure didn't get it from you or
your mother." So many amens,
the smell of boxwood under the June sun

humming through screens. The morning I left
she told me Grandpop had come to see her
during the night. "Do you know
what he said? He said, 'Miz Hammond,

you've kept me waiting long enough.' "
She was, I declare, tickled pink and commenced
blowing me kisses through the bars, bitty
kisses over and over, shooing them along

on her fingers down the hall, dozens
lighting on my shoulders and fluttering
around the corner, down the stairs—
the seventh from the bottom creaking

as it did at 2 A.M. when we were sneaking in,
over the carpets and past the horsehair sofas
cozied with her dolls in the midst of tea—
and out the door, squeezing through the pair

of head-high boxwood grown so abandoned
they almost closed the entrance. Boxwood,

she said, must be trimmed with nail scissors,
each year cutting back the growth,

one piece at a time, like doing
fingers and toes. If left untended
too long, they can't be cut at all.
Such work, love.

Heirlooms Lost

You know how people bury a thing—mostly, it broods,
Tudor-style, walled-off and left to the vines
in some overgrown plot on the moors of the brain, with
one light burning in an upper window.

For two long-lost cousins, the scene of the crime
was an Edenic house in the southern mountains called
Redlands, half-timbered and possessed of an angelic light,
come back from the dead at the sight of each other

standing on a finger pier on a New England waterfront.
He is costumed in foul-weather gear, waiting for the launch.
Their eyes meet, his such a match for the harbor
behind him they seem openings in his head.

Sun tags the water under the pier and sparks fly
between them, up through the gap-toothed boards,
ricocheting like bitten words in a feud so civil
it never happened, mocking the blue sparks that used to fly

at Redlands, decades before the fall, when cousins
played tag after dark in their grandparents' living room,
charging their feet on the Oriental rug, fingers cocked,
loaded with electricity. Now, neither moves,

their feet locked in estrangement not of their making,
while halyards, clanking against aluminum masts,

call like a hundred spoons on goblets for silence
deeper than these years of held fire, deep enough

to hear the cowbells in the pastures at Redlands
from inside the house, where, as evening seeped
down the sky like blueing to meet the mountains,
their two small bodies, warm from baths,

had knelt at the window listening to the herd
carry their swollen udders to the barn. The fat notes
of their bells and low anguish gave them goose bumps
the way the chop of the harbor, glimmering

behind the hero like repoussé, like the sea of silver
that had awaited division on the sideboards and tables
in their grandparents' dining room, does the heroine, now.
Tell me, dear reader, where can our hero turn

but to the sea? Yet, what is there for him
in that direction but a waterscape stolen with mirages
of ill-gotten goods: that hammered sea of roses and daisies,
poppies and pear blossoms, bobbing and sparkling,

lapping against the cloisonné marsh enameled with sun
where the water ripples down into the bas-relief
on the underside of Sandwich glass, that inner harbor
lying flat and sandy-blue as the missing hall carpet,

> > >

seagulls rising off of it as if the tiny birds that cousins
had hunted in the carpet's trees and flowers were flushed
from its warp and woof, that pavé ocean beyond, winking
between dunes, no bigger than a brooch, and lurking

behind it all, the one light burning at Redlands.
Should the cousins speak, the arched front door could creak
open on the night in question. He shifts his weight, appears
to turn toward her. The black iron latch depresses, and

the launch arrives. Without looking back, the hero boards
and, plowing off into the repoussé meadow, illusions
retained, loses body at five knots, enters the dazzle
and vanishes as if it had been he, instead of his mother,

who had crawled on hands and knees out of her old room
into the darkened house, shedding human form as she
wound over Persian carpets from room to room, while
Presbyterian ancestors, wide awake on the walls above,

dreamed on and looked to the next world, as was
this family's wont, varnished eyes full of the elect,
and male heirs, returned gray-haired and balding
to boyhood rooms for their mother's funeral, slept.

Only the narrow dividing of the carpets' pile,
parting and closing, betrayed the creature's glide

through the Persian flora and fauna, filching not only
objects passed honorably from generation to generation,

but, not valuing that her people were American glass
and easily broken, also bearing, with her slide
into the crack of light spilling under her door,
cousins, family, myth, the whole paradise of blindness.

Hubris

1
Communion

Lest we think he's gone, our brother
hangs like Jesus from the dining room wall,
watching over the scrambled eggs and biscuits.
In our father's house it is not necessary
to set a place for him. We all
break bread together. Only the joining
of hands, one with the other, singing grace
around the table, breaks the circle.

Behold. My brother is with me always.
In wedding pictures he's taken for the groom.
We are the couple looking at each other
longer than marriage. We are the ones
holding hands. Look at us, here, starting
down the aisle in the amber light
of time exposures. He's going to give me
away. Rose petals mark the path.
In the gingerbread house clergy await us.
We advance, white-framed, through vaulted ribs
into the forest. Step, hesitate. Squeeze
each other's hand to death. He and I know,
the next time we're here, step, hesitate,
he will be rolled down the aisle.
Mother will want the congregation to sing

"Faith of Our Fathers! Living Still."
Our knuckles show white in every picture.
There are no chicken bones for witches.

So it is, in her nightgown, our mother
offers me a hymnal, her dream folded inside.
It's visited her a dozen times. Before dawn,
she captured it on airmail stationery, meaning
to lift her tidings into my heart, her vision
of a private entrance to a stairway
spiraling up from a dark, stone rotunda
into an airy upper room where everything is white
and very clean, where veils billow from long
windows and fluted pilasters soar into sunbeams.
That I may prepare myself, she wants me
to believe, tucked deep in the black notes
between "Holy Spirit, Truth divine" and "This is
my Father's world," there's an enchanted cottage
complete without a kitchen, no sofas, no chairs,
just two Christmas trees and a high bronze bed.
This is where my brother lives. Up there.
Ahead of us. Waiting. And he's so happy.

He holds out his arms and gathers her in.
Now, she's so happy, she's not afraid of dying.
I haven't the heart to tell her it's a dream,
that he's still in my bed, holding me, promising

me Sparkle Plenty dolls for Christmas,
a Bissell sweeper, a long white dress
with a fingertip veil of illusion,
a toy groom, encompassed by rose petals, left
waiting on the wedding cake.

2
Hubris at White, Ga.

In the end, he was found in remission
200 feet under water, disconnected from his lungs,
proving he didn't need them. Some say
he drank himself down, each 50 feet
into the deep "the equivalent of one dry martini
on an empty stomach," and so swam easy
into us, hands pressed back-to-back reversing
prayer, opening in an arc of benediction,
palms out, begging off, pushing down, denying
angels, flutter-kicking nitrogen into his blood,
happy, happier, the sky shrinking to the size
of a silver dollar until it flipped upside down
through his fingers, fell to the bottom and waited
like an upturned ear listening for his heart

to enter. Which is to say he died laughing,
drowning in euphoria. We have it on film.
We have it in the police report. We also have
two biopsy reports that swear to two other endings.
One reads "Incurable," the other (dated 5 years later),
"Cured." The newsreel doesn't mention them.
That he was taken from us once before and returned.
How, dealt this hand, then this hand, would *you*
accept the deal of a newsreel, an unfathomable

newsreel that has nothing to do with the cards?
Where do you put the newsreel? How do you hold it?
We put it down to a lie—how do you drown
yourself when you know you're going to live?
So, it became an accident, the thought of our brother

in fear, panic, terror at the instant of death
somehow preferable to the thought he was
riddled with unhappiness and cured himself.
An accident, the same way it was an accident that,
three months after the gods wrote "Cured,"
they assigned this brother's brother to film
the drowning. They have him doing 90
down Route 41 in a TV remote-control van, headed
for the quarry and the "Six O'Clock News," not knowing
the "yet-to-be recovered, unidentified male" will be
his brother. He's setting up. He's figuring how
to haul drowning into a camera. Pans of the quarry,
shots of the divers flocking like penguins
tanked with rescue, flippers disappearing into sun,

even recovery, walk on water. He tries
a zoom on the guy's car. Aims. Focuses.
It hurls into him, a collector's rare '47 MG TC,
red. He skids on the sun, blinding the negative,
films the earth slipping stunned out of focus,
chops the heads off trees, tumbles

camera, belly-up to a grip. Weightless,
moonwalks, like Maya Deren, for the close-up,
the confirming wallet on the front seat, our brother's
face, under water, grinning up from his license.
Focus. On pay phone. A mile back. Moonwalk
to reach it. Give desk new angle. Calm, very, say,
"Send me a relief crew." Long-distance,
drop us like stones into the deep. "He's been down

too long." Compressed air has finite boundaries.
Have a seat on the ground. Watch the brother
who's drowning in thin air. Watch him
hug his knees, two fingers hooked
under Speidel, the thumb caressing genies
out of crystal as the shadow sneaks out
of his body, out of the frame, dissolves as the sun
crawls off the water onto the far bank,
collapsing into the woods' neck. Relief crews
fill the fading minutes with tungsten, lock
one camera on the quarry's surface, walk
the other over the farm faces, the scrabbled hands
of the Ladies' Auxiliary, the Red Cross, the spectators
in Monkey Wards and bellies gathering like cows

in Rembrandt lighting on the hillside,
cut away to the floodlit, middle ground
black with silhouettes in wet suits plotting

invasion, bending over math tables, squaring
silver linings with breathing rates, logging
arrivals, departures, the generators packing up
redemption, fueling decompression lines, battling
water with air, loading the divers
like dice. Jump-cut and zoom on the brother's
thumb losing its mind, moving in reverse,
slow motion, counterclockwise, undoing,
unwinding the hours. Frogmen fly in from Texas,
six from Louisiana, land in the foreground
suited for outer space, leave heroic footsteps

and dive deeper into the nectar, into
the chancel of the temple of nitrogen narcosis,
roped in buddies, each pair permitted
one look, one heady dive into the fun house
of omnipotence, one terrible taste of divinity,
then the dirge-slow, decompressing ascent, the surfacing,
their glass faces splintered with water
as if they wept, empty hands banging metal lungs
for air like spoons on a highchair tray.
More air, more air, "mo' beans, mo' beans!"
Cut to brother wiping and wiping his crazed heart
in his sleeve. Oh, Bill, hug yourself
tight. It is Dallas. It is our brother
the diver carries in his arms when he walks,

>   >   >

duck-footed, out of the dark into the living room,
TV lights spilling runny galaxies bobbling
out over the blackened water as he advances,
his wet suit glistening, tattooed with the Milky Way,
cradling a moonshine-freckled twin. The diver
pauses for Atlanta viewers, and two white faces,
one under pressure, one flung free of the earth,
and four hands holding silence, float
in 120 frames of black sequins. The water's edge
waxes, ebbs around the webbed, transmogrified feet
as he's laid on the ground. The sky is unphotogenic;
it doesn't give back the moon, the dumbstruck stars,
our brother. Like flowers, the TV station
sent the outtakes without

the sound clip. Grief composed acknowledgments
in black ink on cream cards, settled an estate,
turned blue, grew goggles, despite itself,
banged for more air. Still, it's taken seven years
to get to this, this look at their condolences,
seven years to pull on flippers, turn out the lights,
enter the outtakes as they washed, 6, 5,
4, 3, the living room wall and, bottoms up, dive
into this sequined silence, this soundless
flickering, float in the absence of chambered
breathing, no bubbling, no heartbeat
pealing in our ears. This is how drowning

is hauled into cameras, the projector humming
longer than held breath, the remaindermen

hanging horizontal, breast-stroking against
gravity in a yellow beam licking the wall until,
lungs bursting, we inhale, loose the angels,
drift to the bottom, hair wafting about our heads,
bodies plumping like wilted greens soaked
in cold water, film slicked over our eyes,
unblinking. Cut! Lights! Sorry. This isn't
the right film. Not like this. No one told him
he would die alive, could die of happiness
outdrinking the gods, lifting his air hose
in a toast, raising it like a third finger,
the sky printing on his eyeballs, he, writing
with his body. Doesn't fool us.
We rehearsed the end a thousand times

for five years. Our hearts are memorized,
covered in greasepaint, camera-ready,
downtown in Roanoke Memorial Hospital,
multiplying, broken like loaves and fishes,
into Humperdinck's fourteen angels. We are with him!
Two are at his right hand, two are at his left,
not to keep him, but to fly along beside, go
half the distance with him, accompanied
by the Mormon Tabernacle Choir

like Margaret O'Brien movies, the way
it's supposed to be, all of us fading
into the white-hot glare, heaven burning off
the pain as we approach. He does not die
"narcked," alone in the dark. Sunspots,

not camera lights, riddle his white
hospital gown, the white sheets holding him,
gobble, like white cells, his translucent face
blue as the oxygen tanks it empties
into, blotting out the border of preachers
in Lifesaver collars he banished at 17, calling them
"Crows!" when they brought him the willies,
flocking in their wing tips to his bedside
to "prepare him," tanked on prayer and the end
as it was written in black and white, not film,
on the biopsy report, standing shoulder-to-shoulder
with doctors shrugging, their hands diving
for the currency of God in lab-coat pockets,
coming up with sand dollars, unopened,

inoperable, two months, two years, at best,
thumbs twiddling time on mustard gas, the dark
jazz of hopelessness: their best offer: his body
carved up, diagrammed with blue crayon
like the butcher's pig, tithed for cracklings
from Cobalt rays and revelations for others.

"Amen," the preachers murmured, circling belief.
I showed them doubt, the hobnail boot of faith,
showed them the angels inside urchins
snapped open like cookies, showed them
the door. Guinea pigs dance
on the point of a very fine needle. They do this
without jostling each other. They do not
need pity or lawyers. Stand-up philosophers

scratch fleas for a living. They pull rungs
out from under the dying, give them medieval
knees, loosen prayer from the eye sockets,
make them weaker than the camel's back.
Tears baptize the gods. They should be
stiffed. Mornings, he was poisoned, gassed,
fried. Afternoons were filled with vomit.
Nights, he took his life back, put it
in his own hands, buckled mine into the seat
beside him, fueled up at Esso,
compressed the odds, pressed us to the floor,
turned the MG to our heads and gunned it,
the highway freezing in our headlights, leaping
from 0 to 60 in 8 seconds, leaving behind

twin streaks of graffiti, hitting 90 and
running without a trace, the engine humming,
clocking our ascent in revolutions per minute,

climbing, the blacktop coiled beyond vision,
our heads whipped back defying cancer, mouths
open clawing the sky, slinging laughter
at the curves, the cliffs, the abyss, rushing up
the mountain to the empty cylinder. At 3 A.M.,
the Appalachians insert plain-faced taverns,
lawless, jut-jawed, between the stars
and the clouds wafting like angel hair at the bottom
of the night. They serve 6-point ale in paper cups,
and jukeboxes, bow-legged with greasy neon
and broken hearts, swell the pine, raw-sawed

walls. Given honest money, the jukebox arm
encircled the Temptations, the Four Freshmen
grown old, the needle leading notes and dust
and our toes to its very fine point.
We twirled and dipped on varnished floors, awash
in smokey lights, our arms roping us like buddies.
But we had substance, we occupied space: sometimes
we danced cheek to cheek, holding, holding,
holding on tight, our feet not moving.
Even when you stop dying, quarries beckon.
They offer some place dark to dance without
jostling, to beg while pretending not to,
to pretend, like a poet, we are godly, alone
on the head of a pin, able to dive to the bottom

>   >   >

and enter the sky, a film's white tail slapping
around, our brother, sprocketted, celluloid, hauled
up, over, down, under, spinning, turning, flap,
flap, flap, flap, flap. Bill
puts his hand on the reel, stills it,
extinguishes the yellow beam. No one
moves. Daddy, like the Angel of Remission,
reaches out, wraps the end back on the spool
and turns on the machine. The projector
hums, rewinding. He flips on its light.
The diver, with the speed of Charlie Chaplin
apologetics, bends down, picks up our brother,
backs, duck-footed, away from us,
into the water and disappears.

3
Accepting the Body

Consider the charms of the water, its weakness,
how, under certain conditions, it grows weary
of the weight of the sky, surrenders,
in times of hushed clarity, its spell,
and ships air. Clouds
float to the bottom, nestle
on the seaweed and sand, drift,
unaltered over the forest

where my brother lies sleeping, his lungs
pricked on a spindle. Minnows and skate
slide through the brambles, the water
everywhere, held back and invisible,
waiting. Gulls swoon on their backs, plummet
crying into the clouds, remember
and backstroke, lie down
with sea robins. Consider

the blessings in bad omens, how they be arrayed
with glory work, the hocus-pocus gestures,
small acts of cleansing, some notion
to scour the kingdom for water and hide it.
The clouds grow up around him, and we,
gifted with no inkling, can tell ourselves

nothing; neither also, do we fall asleep
for a hundred years. Wherefore,

at the hours when the water is off-guard,
least consecrated, most haunted by childhood,
and the sun is hard gold slipped under our boat,
I balance on the gunwale and dive,
my wings firming in the cold descent,
pushing deeper and deeper into the sky,
into the forest, swimming down
into Georgia. This time
I won't wake him.

Praying for Separation

Thank you God for giving my husband half-glasses,
now, as my body begins its descent,
that when we love or draw close for talk,
I lose my imperfections. He says he's blessed
I was presbyopic when we met.
He has a good sense of humor. That,
and this nicely coinciding softening
of visual and physical clarity, make up
a little for the way you give us, at this same hour,
as if they were thieves siphoning our life, daughters
at the peak of hormonal perfectibility who hang on
glittering with 20–20 gnawing hindsight. Agreed,
we let her down. We know our trespasses; we still
have our hearing. And we did promise
kisses would make her feel all better. But

make her go away, anyway. We're tired
of believing our tight fists, her narrow eye.
Spare her further harm from us. Grant
that we be left alone, her father and I, to touch
fingertips as we sit to review the day, to view
ourselves uncorrected as old film stars
photographed through cheesecloth.
And for her to whom we gave cheekbones,
high arches, great teeth and, according to her,
little else, give her what we could not—a font,
a basin, a sea floor for her bottomless heart

that it may catch the rain and fill and fill
until it sounds with the abundant life
her exacting, deep-blue eyes repel. But, then, dear
God, should you grant her this, spare her
a firstborn of such unending hunger that she think
the mother heart sloshes with thin gruel,
that she drown her wish for others in it.

Triptych with Missing Madonna

1

What is this thing they want from me?
A blessing, they call it. They want
my blessing? They turn me upside down and
shake me and shake me as if it were something
I hoarded, something that could fall out
of my insides. One grabs an arm, another a leg,
another my yarn hair. They scream in my face.
Nothing. Not even a rattle. Could there be any
tribute left in this sawdust? Somehow, another
gold charm for her bracelet? Some hour of the day
I withheld? How can they think there's anything
in me worth having and treat me like this?
Did I swallow a tooth when she pulled them?
A button? That eye she yanked off? Maybe
they're trying to help me cough it up. Maybe
if I unstitch my lips, open my grin, whatever it
is will drop out, and my painted smile will fall
off. Maybe that's what they want. Or,

maybe they just like breaking their toys.
They must know if I had a blessing left in me,
it would pop out, as always? Happily.
Anything to get her to stop shaking me.
It hurt so that she had to. But she did.
A lot. I'm slow, you see, never could

give fast enough, often enough, much enough.
Patterns. Like the one I was cut out of
following the chalk outline left
in the intersection. You get used to things,
adapt. The bell rings, the dog drools.
Otherwise, no use calling attention to yourself.
Bad, bad mommy. All the same, the teensiest shake,
the itsiest pout, and bingo, it was hers,
anything, to stop the reminder I was unreal.
She'd pull up an eyelid, tug on an arm, and I'd go
IloveyouIloveyouIloveyouIloveyou
and flop back splat on the floor.

2

You can't blame her for getting aggressive.
She's so used to automatic delivery she thinks
I'm a vending machine. Swat! Klang! *IloveyouIloveyouIloveyou*
Swat-swat-swat! double-Klang! KaPLOOey!
Uh, wrong recording. I'm supposed to prove my love.
Give her an apartment. Without roommates.
Requiring roommates constitutes abandonment.
I show her my pockets. Bad Mommy.
*Pockets with nothing in them constitute
conditional love.* (I think I should find
what mafiosos make *her* recordings.)

She beams her brimming eyes out on the world
and saints rush to the rescue, the better,
they say, for helping her kick me: first,

her boyfriend's parents buy her a house, so there!
To keep her in. While keeping their boy
home with them. Because they are Christian,
they say, so, double there! and send a ransom note;
next, my parents (a whole other story) furnish
the house, so there! Because they are gen-u-ine
Christians, they say, so, double there! Besides,
I have the wrong thoughts, so, triple there!
So now, all these better people are shaking me,
screaming, *Your blessing! Your blessing!*
We want your blessing! If my adding machine
still works, this comes to eleven people in all,
counting peripheral characters, who want me to prove
my love, seven of whom I don't even like. Splat.

   3

It wasn't always like this. I used to be one
heck of a woman back when I was a lumberjack
and timbered the Daddy Tree before he could fall
on me. His limbs kept dropping down on my head,
klunk, klunk, boing. *Timber!* I yelled

and floated him down the river to the sawmill.
I was quicker and faster when I was alive.
I thought *that* was a blessing, but she hated it.
That's when the shaking began. She shook me enough
for two trees. A good hard shaking for the Daddy Tree
for having loose limbs, and one for me for not
giving him back, anyway, when she said
she'd protect me if I would, didn't I remember
how she tried. I figured this was good for her
and what I deserved. I understood people
who needed to hurt the wrong person back.
And I was all she had. I could take it;
I loved my little seedling, my angry sprout.

Isn't it amazing what we'll do for our child
to see ourselves canonized? She wanted a mommy;
I wanted to be chiseled in marble. So she shook.
And I smiled and tossed my hair like oak leaves.
And she shook. Oh, I'd be more than enough for her.
And she shook. And I delivered as if my arms
were many branches. And she shook. And my bark
fell off, and the limbs fell bare, and put out
no new shoots, and they hauled me off to the sawmill.
But I did leave instructions to put the remains
in a look-alike Raggedy Ann, something she could
push in her buggy, drag around by the neck, tuck
in the crook of her dreams between thumb and blanket,

so she'd feel secure, not know the difference.
I mean I was doing the best I could.
But you can't fool kids. She's so mad I let her
kill me, she's not going to stop
until she finds my candy heart and eats it.

Maybe that's a blessing.

World Without End

My spanky Daddy. Always, you call it
helping, your hands flashing to your waist,
fingers blurring like lawn-mower blades, and
slash, leather rips from belt-loops,
crazed, climbs the air overhead
coiling. Always, I disappear. I am not

your teeny daughter in hand-smocked dresses
your Mamma sent, my pretty new dresses
with sashes cut off, your scissors
raging through my closet so everyone
can see, until the hems can be let down
no further, my badness,

the stubs of my sashes sticking out
like baby arms chopped off. Even grown, I am not
your daughter when you're detaching my daughter,
year by year, snip by snip, enticing her
to come sit down beside you, snuggle, bring you
all her problems with me

as if she were a sash and yours to wield
like a belt on my bare heart, spanking
Mommy until I'm embroidered with welts,
smocked and ruched, with stubs
sticking out, my mother arms
chopped off. I am, as always, your

> > >

mother and your father and your wife.
And you hit them and hit them
and hit them. After, you feel
so much better, so cheerful, so pained,
vouchsafed and holy, that I know I am
you, and it is good

I was a brave, stout-hearted, little boy
shedding not a tear. And I sit down beside you,
snuggle, happy for you, and cover you
with kisses, listening to you, snip by snip,
warn me off *my* mother. Oh, yes, Daddy,
this is love.

Open Season

Postmark: Peterborough, NH, Oct. 25, 198__

The mailboxes here are open pigeonholes,
homemade yellow-pine crannies, oiled
with the rub of the near and the famous,
reaching. I want, first, to give you
the look of it, have you see how your letter
blessing my escape and wishing me poems
landed in this artists' sanctuary in the aftermath,
as you knew, of months of perfectly good words
flying off the family tongue so mean
blackbirds rolled upside down on the phone lines
playing 'possum from New York to Florida, words
flying so ugly they came back reincarnated as
black flies dancing from one wing to the other with
ink they can't hold any longer, so they don't,

bursting bold-faced in yellow cablegrams, all caps,
        "YOUR DEEP-SEATED INFERIORITY
        COMPLEX . . . ,"
foaming at the mouth of ball-point pens,
        ". . . proof of your twisted need to control. . . ,"
squirting from the nibs of fountain pens,
        ". . . demonstrated by the insult of your warped . . ."
psssting from behind plain brown wrappers,
        ". . . refusal to mind, forces us to do . . ."
licking the lead of their pencil stubs,
        ". . . you! know! what!"

without once remembering to unzip, when
all else failed, words, relieving themselves
in the tulips on Mantovani stationery, crooning,
"Stand Up, Stand Up for Jesus," and
"Nobody Knows De Trouble I Seen."

You can see, in such a case, how kindness
might lean slant in a pigeonhole, might look
like one white wing waiting to flutter
when the fingers touched it, how it might seem thin
and still release the feathers family plucked,
how it might seem the juice of thigh meat
the aforementioned-whose-names-I've-forgotten sucked.

What you couldn't know because I bragged
how well all goes with poems here shielded
from family, was the way tears came, finally,
to slit open my nights and crows flew
from my belly pecking the eyes out of my dreams,
couldn't know sleep heaved the tombstones
covering the damned up to the surface,
and my fingers read their carved names
remembering, that then, I couldn't get sleep
back in the envelope, and if I didn't
there'd be no words for the A.M. and flies
on the living daylights, and I didn't, and
there weren't, and so on, you get the picture:

> > >

by the third week of putting so many
perfectly good words out of my mind,
I was crouched night and day in my head
not getting a bead on even a comma, when
here's your letter perched in my pigeonhole (easy,
sometimes a pigeonhole is just a pigeonhole),
and it's not taking a leak, it's practicing
continence, the first piece of mail in months
I don't have to put on a waterproof slicker to read
wiping my eyes with toilet paper. You can

imagine my loss of gravity holding a piece
of pure white 20 lb. Bond containing
no words to define me, the updraft
beholding perfectly good words not aiming
to thrash me, wing me, or, in lieu of
the direct hit, burgle, con, mastermind, or
erase me, just words, laundered of all trace
of the hustle associated with cement-shoe salesmen
looking for customers, words, again,
swift and translucent as a watercolor
drawing the paper's texture into the picture,
as a poem writes the white space, as
The Wall Street Journal clip you enclosed
"for inspiration," headlined "Wild Turkeys
Spot Hunters Before They Can Get Off A Shot"
flushed the poet under siege into takeoff:

Hunting for Words

Dateline: Turkey Mountain, USA, October 8, 198___

Writers are sleepless and empty-handed.
Words have become hard to flush as wild turkeys.
Worse, the ratio of words to writers has reached
one-to-one, and words are getting smarter.
Nature's way is to select against
the dumb bird. In some areas, words
have even stopped gobbling to avoid detection.
A word can spot a poet at 200 yards and—

with the footspeed of a sprinter and the ability
to fly 50 miles an hour—disappear in an instant.
Accordingly, some poets, instead of wearing
the Day-Glo colors worn by other writers
to keep from getting shot themselves, are going to
new lengths in camouflage: in quest of their
elusive quarry, they're signing up for workshops
and Bigger Game tutorials as never before,

with the Orvis system for bagging words,
complete with woodsy shooting galleries and
recorded turkey calls, being set out on upward of
400 campuses, where, to better their odds,
poets practice a noun's repertoire of clucks,
gobbles, and yelps and gather tips on

how to imitate fighting words by beating
arms against legs to lure curious verbs, while

three shotgun manufacturers have fashioned
specialized weapons with camouflaged slings
and no-shine barrels. It helps to be
a little crazy. Poets sit motionless
for hours, every sense alert, unable to think
about black flies, extortion rates, family,
moral runts, lunch, hoping for a few
precious seconds to take aim at a word.

They arise before dawn to call mating yelps
to words, who often wake up in the morning
with sex on their minds. And, poets who stalk,
rather than sit, learn to distinguish the word's
j-shaped droppings. Sadly, today's poets are in
greater peril than words are, what with armed poets
wearing camouflage sneaking up on other poets
wearing camouflage crouching armed and gobbling.

Of course, you and I know I am also the wild turkey
holed up in these woods, hard to flush as words, camouflaged
and getting smarter, the wild turkey family would kill
to get a bead on, the turkey losing her voice
to avoid detection. Today, the season opens
outside. Gunfire lands soft around the afternoon.

Your "regards" are tucked in my manuscript
but I want you to see all of us here, the way
we were last night, flocked in this sanctuary,
"family" and possible, listening by firelight to jigs
Andy Teirstein fiddled to Sister Bernetta's lilt,
all of us, whole and aloft, flying somehow
to a steady-enough beat on one wing,
the memory of the other moving
inside our paintings, our music,
our sculpture, the stories and poems,
this poem, this wing,
you sent, lent,

lifting me rising, soaring across the page,
until the remembered look of it, of kindness
leaning in a pigeonhole, crumples the sky under my hand,
pitching my gobble off-key, and I plummet, sobbing
like a human, so far does your instinct
for arriving at another's place
reach down into me, slant,
standing in for others.

All our growing up Jesus lived in our house
like one of those life-size, headless,
cardboard figures impoverished Victorians
posed behind, borrowing impossible finery
for photographs. We called His name
Father for it was your face and clerical collar
atop His neck, your tongue gutting us
with scorn and disgust and twisted logic
for that which you were about to do:
break our bodies in remembrance of Him.

We worshiped You, four little towheads,
all in a row, all bent double, hands on knees,
receiving the daily blessing of Your belt
to help us, which You promised was serving us
right, which You promised we'd asked for, which
You promised hurt You more, our bare buttocks
turning red as blood around white welts, because
you promised, You were good, so almighty
good You even claimed our pain: You suffered
that we might not, and we loved You
as we could not love ourselves, with a love
that passeth all understanding, understanding
You knew not what You did, thereby
forgiving You, thereby protecting You
from finding out, afraid You'd die
if You knew You were not doing good,
if You knew You broke our insides

when You were drunk on Jesus, afraid we
would die if you stopped: what being had we,
that's mentionable, if we weren't "forgiving"

always unasked; what being had you if you asked?
I'd even forgiven you for stealing the face
of God from me, on top of any inner resource;
there were always newer lashings to forgive,
thank god; it was the only power I had, that and
never telling; the alternative was
separation, death as we are for both of us.
Whose arms were strong enough to hold you up
if we took away the skirts of Jesus? Whose head,
what heart, what arms for us if we gave up You?

But again you steal my child for Jesus,
this time the metaphor made flesh, the child
of my womb, of my heart, a child I could love,
waiting until she was luscious with my sweat
and sleepless nights, ripe with rebellion
for the plucking, filled with damnation
for not giving her this, for not giving her that,
scared of uncoupling. You began unbuckling,
saying, *Fear not,*

for I am with you; My rod and My staff,
My wallet and My pity, shall comfort her, for I am
buying her all that she wants; I am feeding

her righteousness for your own good;
this hurts Me more than you but you
asked for it; you will not listen; you will not
do as I say; if you wish to speak to her again
you will speak My language, for I am creating her
in My own image to serve you right,
for not going to church, for turning
to heathens when you had God, or Me;
I am restoring her soul; I am leading her into
My pastures, for the Fifth Commandment really means
only parents worthy of being honored should be honored;
she shall not want for anything; I'll teach you
a lesson you'll never forget; I'll get you
back into the fold; I'll show you what for!

My collapse, I am told, just goes to prove
I'm a poor loser. And no Christian. Or else
I'd get back on my feet and come with her, cleave
unto the father, unto the daughter, forever,
prop both of them up. Yea, his belt and coiled logic
have followed me all the days of my life until
he's hit me so hard he's knocked off
his head; all the holier-than-Thou-
and-him, hot-air nobility, all
the excusing, that which was
the body of us,
whiffs out the top of my neck.

I am a recovering Jesus,
dead to the old ways, living under a new law
unbuckling, recoiling, drying out
from my father, from my daughter possessed.

II

Exile

Cosmetics

. . . see the music, hear the dance.—GEORGE BALANCHINE, 1904–1983

Cremation? Honey, you've got to be kidding.
Where I come from we lay them out, paint their faces
with the cosmos, and fling back the lid. Some people
believe in the resurrection of the body.
The one you're in. You're not coming back
as Marilyn Monroe. But you are coming back. Worms
steer wide of Christians. Come the Judging,
the winner of the swimsuit division will cry
and say all the contestants have been
perfect angels. First prize is a trip to the moon.
Make sure they put you in clean underwear.
And hang on to your organs. Of course,
your heart will be useless. By law,
arteries and veins are given a good rinse.

No matter what you've heard, it's not true.
The dead do not look wonderful. They do not
look peaceful. Or natural. Ditto, asleep, napping,
serene, resting, relieved, better off, or happy.
They look like they're trying to get out of the coffin.
Don't listen to the preacher, Nellie. The dead aren't
off making celestial hay or running Morgan Stanley.
If those streets were paved with gold,
would they be turning blue under their makeup,
bearing down, laboring, every muscle
braced with determination, waiting
for the surge of adrenaline to make them

levitate, as if holding our breath ever got us
anywhere, ever kept any lid from lowering?

Look at those cowboy messengers, dreaming
of Mercury on top of the world running
with his body. Study that attitude, their attack
on death, their string ties. The high-minded,
the seemly, won't be seeing the tergiversations
at the bottom of the box, the legs crossing,
one foot over the other, or the feet flopping over,
flexed, like propellers (or butterfly wings
if the feet be small), in first position. Dreamers
need the magnolias we tuck in their hands, and we
need to kiss them good-bye as if they were
themselves, as if the coldness will not enter
memory like formaldehyde, give it the taste
of satin and frogs, of god forbid, ashes.

O, Georgians, push up from the diaphragm.
Attitude! Attitude! For Balanchine's Requiem,
baby ballerinas rose from the corps, flew
from the wings with long necks, arms and legs
flashing across the moon holding on Central Park,
and came down without chalk marks at the Cathedral
of Our Lady of the Sign in high heels and dresses,
loose hair, landing in third position,
arms exiled behind their backs, weighty

as Degas's bronzed *Little Fourteen-Year-Old Dancer*.
Even in that ballroom converted to sanctuary,
they hid inside the faces of cosmeticians, sweating
and crying like anyone. But their toes, unmasked
in sandals, I swear, were knobbier than mortals'.

Unbelievers, it's hands, not feet, we paint
to match the face, fold them on Byzantine chants
in the final port de bras as if they'd retired
from the classroom, never to mold another
battement tendu, blind to the universe
singing in the curl of magic swung by priests
dabbing perfume on the air, sending the night,
silken as Monte Carlo, to shimmy Georgian
above the aspirations of burning candles,
sprinkling a serenade into the ballerinas' feet
snapping open in first position, carrying them
single file, bobbing like ducklings in tutus
up to the casket, out onto the lake, sinking,
one by one into curtain curtsies, their thin arms

escaping the borders of the body, rearranging
space. Rising, they kissed the face and hands,
the prayer band on the forehead, tears watering
symmetry, lips tasting the powder of the tomb, wings
fluttering behind them like Odette, wings rolling away
the stars, dusting Lazarus's cave, Apollo's stairway,

making ready departure, lift-off. And, on the third day,
yes, ma'am, at six past eight, the conductor
tapped his baton, the sky rolled up like a scroll,
the body arched, the head lifted, the shoulders
dropped, elongating the neck, and the arms, unfolding
in three connected movements, took second position,
flowed into third, each hand wrapping gravity,
saucy around its little finger, the spirit rippling

down through the thighs, the clenched calves,
curving into the satin toe box, stepping, piqué,
onto fourth, and with one leg letting go of the earth,
bent back at the knee, one arm reaching up, it entered,
against a gelatin sky, the fouetté en tournant, circling
the linoleum, every limb whipping air into the torso,
spinning, harder, faster, pushing up, until,
amen, the body rose, the ballerina's wrists
bending heaven, fingers flicking it away, legs
hyphenating space, one pointed toe catching our heart
sightseeing down the cheek like a missed beat
or a rebel moon, and fixing it somewhere
out in the galaxy of the Fifth Ring, between the dark
geometry of the music and the choreography of the corps.

Slow Dancing in the Living Room, Thanksgiving

Funny the way the healing comes
in a northeaster, rain sliding
sideways across the glass, the waves
beaching themselves, rolling home
across the gray water, running before the wind
boxing the spruce and cedars fat with resistance.

Russian olive and beach plum,
stripped to their bird-bone branches
blackened with rain against the still-
green lawn, jerk and twitch, stiff
with cold, offering so little
to the blow, they bend, barely.

Even from the bay window, clouds
are near, putting a ceiling on the sky
trying to slip off the water through a slit
of dove-gray on the horizon. Only
gulls are nervy enough to fly
in this weather. They, too, slide

sideways, behind the rain, wings
spread wide grabbing the currents
and sledding across the wind as if
they were made for a northeaster, designed
all gray with flashes of white
to match its color. Banking,

> > >

they turn into the wind and wobble,
their backsides to us, heading away, small,
unsteady as a child learning to walk
the hard way. Inside—all the things God gives
that were always there, all that's man-made
keeping us, the light bulbs, glowing

through yellowed parchment shades,
converting a 17th-century day, filling in
the shadow of our daughter, the fire
toasting the room, Gershwin and Porter
coming from Public Radio in a braid
of complicated notes, a music written

before we were born, surviving in a changed
world, and this good man holding me, I
holding him, as we glide in Top-Siders
across the rug, seeing each other return
sliding sideways into our eyes
this side of the glass.

Ecumenical Movements on a Coffee Table

We were buying redleaf lettuce and arugula
from the Korean greengrocer to give us a
leg up on outliving, by two to three months,
ourselves, when we spotted the tulips,
yellows, whites, orange-y pinks, and blood reds,
which sit, now, like colors from a crayon box,
in a white Wedgewood notion of a Grecian urn
on the coffee table surrounded by mounds of books—
Wordsworth and The Age of English Romanticism;
Larkin; Lessing; Bettelheim; Berke's *Tyranny of Malice:*
The Dark Side of Character and Culture; a roll
of dice canted on the *Daedalus* issue on Eastern Europe—
and, oh, how, with a copper penny dropped in the water
for longevity, the way a drop of gin
brings lilacs back, they arch, penetrating space
vertically like steeples, diagonally like dancers
rising in slow motion, the stems, tensing with
gulped water, lifting, straightening, yes, craning
up into the darkened living room
as if they were inhabited by the holy ghost,
transmitted by satellite from the squares of Timisoara,
Budapest, Prague, Crakow to small-screen television,
of this rolling away of the stone,
this new thrust away from despots
charged by the ions of Caesar's coin.

Juncture

FOR KATHERINE

For weeks after the discovery, you looked for
likable answers, too shamed to call, too numb to cry.
When you did ring, it was my "Hello?," you said,
straight from our adolescence, that found your tears.
Once we had a Magic Eight Ball, unlimited local calls,
and all the answers. Gradually, we've come to loving,
long-distance, as best we can. "Yes," I can provide
beds to break your family's trip from Boston

to your daughter in recovery. "Yes," New York is soft
with eight inches of snow. At dinner, in candlelight,
we lift our glasses, hesitate. *No,* one hardly drinks
to Julia, hospitalized for treatment, a teenage alcoholic,
even though leukemia might give her better odds.
Your mother, too, goes without saying.
Our husbands save the moment: "To Edith Hamilton,
Greek scholar, revisionist, founder of the school

that brought you two together." Earlier,
I made us go for a walk. It was no accident
we passed the Guggenheim, its rotations
against the white trees and sidewalks
as invisible as the angels that children
imprint in snow. I wanted you to have a souvenir
for the next leg of your trip, a vision
of the unexpected way the spirit swoops down

>   >   >

and up. I wanted you to see the Reservoir, too,
where skyscrapers and lace forests float
like tea leaves, but two-thirds of it was gone,
riddled with sun, the radiance consuming
Central Park South, most of the West Side as well,
the way denial grows on love, the way it happened
that you were blinded to the eyes in your daughter's
15-year-old face, the same endless blue

that guarded your mother's face as she died in binges
without revisioning. Oh, Kappy, the doubling for you!
Here, where we're tired, and settled in our stories,
you're forced with sight to rework yours.
Once more answers rise in the Eight Ball,
once more the happenstance to refigure loving,
your daughter, your mother, up close,
from a long distance.

Suffrage

FOR ANNE

I went to *The Bostonians* last night and thought
of you and your body cast, the way the filmmakers
corsetted, like orthopedic surgeons, the heroine's
body until it pouted, made flesh the hourglass
woman's time runs through. Falling off a horse
and breaking your back has its advantages: you can
lie in bed, stare at the ceiling, twiddle your thumbs,

and never see history squirm when the heroine
is shot in profile with the bones of whales
needed to suppress her nipples, never see the pain
of two half-moons, tideless and safe as mother,
that rise to the level of meringues, jewelry,
or a noose. Does it hurt very much, this de-
naturing? When your husband clasps his hands

around the pillar of your waist, rigid,
unbending, holding himself as he never dreamed,
where do you go? Flicked like a belly-up beetle,
can you feel the footprints shriveling inside?
Sure, you're lucky to be alive, lucky paralysis
is temporary. And, that time may pass quickly,
think of yourself as our grandmothers

saved from the past. May each month of bondage
mark a decade of theirs. Live in your corset
as if it were their lives, so you may rush, as

they could not, through sixty years in six months.
Be glad you can arise from the casket. Be glad
your life awaits you. Be glad you'll be up
in time to vote. Tell us about time.

Making Breakfast

There's this ritual, like a charm,
Southern women do after their men
make love to them in the morning.
We rush to the kitchen. As if possessed.
Make one of those big breakfasts
from the old days. To say thank you.
When we know we shouldn't. Understanding
the act smacks of Massah, looks shuffly as
all getout, adds to his belly, which is bad
for his back, and will probably give him
cancer, cardiac arrest, and a stroke. So,
you do have to wonder these days as you
get out the fat-back, knead the dough,
adjust the flame for a slow boil,
flick water on the cast-iron skillet
to check if it's ready and the kitchen
gets steamy and close and smelling
to high heaven, if this isn't an act
of aggressive hostility and/or a symptom
of regressed tractability. Although
on the days we don't I am careful
about broiling his meats instead of
deep-fat frying them for a couple of hours,
dipped in flour, serving them smothered
in cream gravy made from the drippings,
and, in fact, I won't even do
that anymore period, no matter what

he does to deserve it, and, besides, we are
going on eighteen years so it's not as if we
eat breakfast as often as we used to,
and when we do I now should serve him—
forget the politics of who serves whom—
oatmeal after? But if this drive answers
to days when death, like woolly mammoths
and Visigoth hordes and rebellious kinsmen,
waited outside us, then it's healthy, if
primitive, to cook Southern. Consider it
an extra precaution. I look at his face,
that weak-kneed, that buffalo-eyed,
Samson-after-his-haircut face, all of him
burnished with grits and sausage
and fried apples and biscuits and my
power, and adrift outside himself,
and the sight makes me feel all over
again like what I thank him for
except bigger, slower, lasting, as if,
hog-tied, the hunk of him were risen
with the splotchy butterfly on my chest,
which, contrary to medical opinion, does not
fade but lifts off into the atmosphere,
coupling, going on ahead.

Blessings

1.

My Mother-in-Law Sailing

Her heart fails her and the body holding it
lies on its side, the lungs taking on fluid
so it will be, we are told, like drowning
we can't stop and each week's watch is a hot
potato we relay over Nantucket Sound rotating
by ferry in partial acceptance full steam ahead
from Woods Hole to the Vineyard and back
like boats on moorings, the buds on trees
at each landfall swelling, halyards banging
and banging aluminum masts,

the hull of her tippy, gaff-rigged Sneakbox
reassembling from rot, its rudder tugging
loose from coffee table legs, the mast
floating, cradled in cobwebs, down
from the Boathouse rafters, drifting
dreamy, end over end toward the hull,
its foot settling in the step, ready
for the sail's climb and
blossoming, its
lifting of the boat through the water
maybe on a beam reach, or running
before the wind, something full and easy
enough for the boom to lift and dip a bit
in air just right for benediction.

\>   \>   \>

It will be a clear day and the sky will be white
all the way to the horizon
and blue at the top,
with no spit of beach beckoning
under the shorn hills and scrubby pine,
with no landfall,
the strum of the water in the tiller,
and "Tea for Two," or "Wild Flower" on the Victrola.

2.

Second Sight

The congestive heart takes the extremities first
and recent memory, the result
of oxygen diminution. The patient's slow drift
up to the womb begins with visions of bugs
it is not given to us to see, swarming
the walls of this world, followed,
in Ethel's case, as if dying ran a hot iron
over invisible ink, by the wish
to tell her mother good night.

It's a gift, the averted mind, indeed a blessing,
the way the code materializing, the past outshining
the present, gives offspring sight of the mother
untwined from them, and sight of themselves
on earth but not in her eyes, their world as it will be.
A blessing, too, the way it gave Ethel company
beyond us: her Fraülein and Mrs. Eddy,
her mother's mustachioed laundress—she could hear
the rustle of their petticoats; we could see
how small her gestures became—her parents'
neighbors she never knew she knew, and
the return to her side of some man in green trousers
who, maybe, was, and, maybe, wasn't, a likeness
of the man in green trousers in the silver frame

on her bureau. Such a comfort he was,
although she couldn't think why. Nor
could she think why she'd be so queer
as to have a photograph of a stranger.

And, certainly it was a blessing the way
her withdrawing made it easy to avert our hearts,
except for those bugs and "that couple,
darn them, oh, you know their names,
intrusive, perfectly horrid pair! Told me,
the nerve! I was dying, and jumbled the dials
on my oxygen machine!" We made ourselves real.
We swatted her bugs, talked to her Fraülein,
kicked out that couple, day after day dusting
good riddance off our hands, stood spread-eagle,
flexed, bracing the door with our backs.
They oozed through wood, our flesh, her brain,
fiddling and jumbling and fiddling.

So much for the favors of oxygen deprivation.
Extremities bluing, circulation dwindling, the creep
of starved nerves dying, the cold crawling toward
the lungs filling, these are the heart's turf.
High summer and we closed windows, lit fires,
turned her electric blanket up to 10. Still,
her hands and feet hurt so much she wanted
rid of them. "Outgrown shoes and gloves,"

we sang, and huffed and puffed removing them,
slung her pain in the trash believing
we could make her believe; they flew up
out of the trash back on. Tighter than before.
And tighter. And tighter. The night she swore
someone in white was behind her, the last
pocket of air was diminishing, and there wasn't
room between the headboard and wall for an angel,
but someone was there and she knew it,
why did we pretend there wasn't,
had we forgotten she hated surprises!

The medical profession reverted to pronouns:
"It's near. She's begun. She's making
those movements they make at the end." And Ethel's
daughter in tennis whites climbed into the bed where
she was conceived, tucked herself along her mother,
rocking her through time. The rest of us, flicked
with candlelight, sat at the foot of mother and child,
their reverse pietà, and those movements,
the involuntary grimaces scrunching up,
stretching, and contorting her face, the ceaseless
curling and opening of hands, that one arm
aloft and bent, laden with muscle and bone mass,
elbowing the night, holding death at bay,
while her feet and legs fished the sheets as if,
tiring in the deep of her mother's sea, she

searched for bottom, or the rung of a ladder.
There were sounds. Of sucking in
the wrap of the planet. Of not.

The fetus, with no memory of suckling,
finds its thumb in the fifth month.
We don't know why. Nor is it certain
why for weeks the primitive systems of infants
appear to recall the amniotic environment.
Days before she left us, Ethel's two grandnephews
arrived, were held up by the heels, drew breath,
and turned pink with the increase in oxygen,
days after were brought to us for viewing,
and we tucked them into our arms and the crooks
of our necks and slipped into the mother-sway,
standing and swaying, sitting and swaying,
chatting and swaying, weight sliding through
our hips, antiphonal, reflexive, accompanying them.
This is the way they will rock their mothers, as
distanced by the crepy flesh from reckoning

as we, faced with the pearly skin of infants, were,
ohhing and ahhing at the involuntary grimaces
scrunching up, flitting across their tiny faces,
cooing over their minute hands, unleavened
by muscle and bone mass, drifting like milkweed
on the summer air, curling and opening,

laughing at the dream of the breast
working their jaws in a spasm of nursing, withal
that their legs, under wisps of blankets, still
molded in the fetal position, were fishing
for this life, for the feel
of the planet under them, were climbing,
unseeing as plants to the sun,
back into those movements we make
as we leave one world and are born to the next.

3
Paying Respects

Our fourth night of being, her children
and I, alone in her house without her,
she was returned from the mainland
after hours for the cemetery, and so
her two sons collected her at the ferry
and brought her back for one last night,
setting her down on the cobbler's bench.
We ignored her as if she were there.
At her usual bedtime her elder son
carried the cardboard box into her room
and sat it in the middle of the made bed.

Both were early risers and before anyone
was up he slipped downstairs in his robe,
tucked the box in the crook of his arm,
and walked to the beach the way her legs
couldn't this last year, sitting on the steps
watching the water materialize. From there
he traveled all their conjoint projects
in her fifteen years of widowhood, over all
her earthly domain, bearing the ashes
around to the boathouse, off through marsh grass
to the pond to review the erosion, through
deep sand to the point and the ospreys' nest, on

to the new section cleared of bittersweet,
and back, in the spreading light, to the driveway,
the dormers over the garage, the basement
to inspect the new hot water tank,
the settings for the lawn sprinkler system,
before walking, room by room, through her house,
each with its fading wallpaper from her own
mother's reign, lingering at the thresholds
of her sleeping middle-aged children, ending
in the parlor where she presided mornings,
putting the box down, while he went to dress,
on her place on the sofa. He omitted,
his sister was sure when she saw the box there,
the inflexible part of their mother's routine.
She scooped it up and ran, the vaguely
hostile son calling out, "Don't forget to put
the lid down first," both of them pouring cereal
giggling, fidgeting, hearing a burst of laughter
when he found her, both swooping off
to the john to join him, all three laughing,
leaning against the tiles, until they cried.

When it was time to leave for Tower Hill
we waited in the Buick trying not to see him
standing on the knoll with the box
taking a last look at Nantucket Sound,
trying not to see him, when he turned,

this gangling, aging boy and his Mamma,
offer his arm, trying not to see him,
bending slightly to her height and weight,
pat the place on his forearm and tuck it
close. At her pace, they proceeded
away from the sea to her English garden,
nodding and bowing in succession
to the zinnias, the marigolds, the roses,
the hollyhocks, bowing and bowing
to dahlias, asters, Marguerites, phlox,
thanking and thanking.

Nefertiti

. . . when I shall begin the great poems of my middle period.

—LOUISE GLUCK

Having invested 34 centuries, 17
cooking vessels, 2 female servants,
3 cats in jeweled collars, 4 bronze
and enamel chamber pots, 5 jars
of Visible Difference, 8 bags
of commemorative coin, 1 clove of garlic,
and 10 spare teeth in an afterlife,
we can imagine her befuddlement when
she turned up instead, above ground
among the Christians, a tourist—
as who isn't in the first months back—
standing with prison pallor in the sand
outside her summer pyramid in shorts
and a pair of Jellies from Latin America.
It is not known whether she died
without warning or was just wool-gathering
the last 30 seconds before death, but
she missed the rerun of her life
and considered herself fortunate. Now
her past awaits her. First, there is
the pyramid itself. It took 340 slaves
and 9 overseers 3 years to cover the exterior
with gray shingles. Otherwise
New England Revival would have had to wait
2 centuries after the discovery of America.
The door opens, creaking like Sunday night
on the radio and she breathes
mildew. Here are the great poems

of her middle period: in the bedroom,
"Curtains" made on her mother's Singer,
her knee pressing the throttle, eliminating
the awkwardness of pricking her finger
and being kissed awake by Prince Charming
in the missionary position when she's 116 years old;
next, "Bedspread in Checks," created 1 year
before gingham and money were the rage,
its unrelenting rhythm, a harbinger
of the return to the classical tradition
as noted in the issue on Appalachian Cheek
in *Le Dernier Cri de la Mode Dur;*
then (a word she's not fond of
because of its connotations), "Crumbs"
fallen between the cracks of the sofa
from the mouths of certain so-called
adults in the grip of terminal excusitis
dementia brought on by emotional retardation,
and left there because they were thought
to attract mice. Of course, some crumbs
were fallen from the mouths of people
who did not want to sit at the same
dinner table with other people, the very
table which was the inspiration for
the overheated "Dinner Party #99" worked
in the whimper-whimper-bang anapests
of the Grateful Dead jamming with the
dactyls of Coltrane in which could be seen

new breeding grounds for nuclear fission.
Also under the sofa cushions were "Homework,"
"Hockey Pucks," "Lost Sleep," "Broken China,"
"Curfews Ignored," "Sour Grapes," "Expletives
Deleted," "College Applications," "Spilled Milk,"
"Loose Change," and "A Couple of Marbles,"
the remains of a daughter, all
from the C-section of her oeuvre called
The Princess and Her Paupers. And, there,
tossed on top, lie the famous "Prickly Pillows,"
needlepointed with one word stabbed
in and out of the canvas. Certainly, the colors do
pull the room together but if we could read
her mind we might guess she were wishing
she'd had the "flash before your eyes and
be done with it" experience instead;
coming back has its side effects, like
feelings flooding in with no place to go, as if,
seeing the artifacts of a prior dynasty, she
stood viewing her own body she can't rejoin.
Except on the table in the bay window
sits the blank writing tablet abandoned
a millennium back. As these things go,
there's a stylus waiting. It's left to her
to begin the late poems of her early period,
the happy poems of resurrection running
ahead of her small death.

Snowbound in a Summer House
off the Coast of Massachusetts

Wind registered on my eardrums like high altitude,
popping my eyes open on the dark. I listened
to keep the roof on, deaf to the snow's spit
lashing the windows and sticking. At 6 A.M.
the phone: "Evacuate! That wind is serious.
Those waves are serious. This snow is serious.
By afternoon, the wind chill factor aims to freeze
exposed skin in 30 seconds and
the nearest human is a mile and a half away.
Now! Or you're on your own."
I have no hat. I have no boots. No
four-wheel drive. My Italian leather gloves
with French seams are Sunday-go-to-church
and my own seams seemed stitched in Romania.
It sounded like perfection to me.
And the covers felt like heaven. So.
"We have to think of the pipes," I said.
"They might freeze. Someone might have to
drain the system, or keep the fireplaces up."
"You don't understand, this is life-threatening!"
"*You* don't understand," the hillbilly in me said
before the phone went dead, "that's just the point."

Every window is iced as a Hallmark card, what's
outside, invisible and desperate as its sentiment.
I have 2 cans of tuna, 6 eggs,
4 slices of oatmeal bread,

1 can of Campbell's Golden Mushroom, and
hot chocolate for a week. I have studied
the plumbing system. I don't know
what I'm seeing but I've looked at it.
I've filled the bathtubs with water. By afternoon
the woodpile will be more than 30 seconds
from the house. I've lugged in enough logs
to make 4 fireplaces roar 24 hours.
Less than enough, actually, but my less
admirable side, call it La-dee-dah Belle, as in
"those Yankee gentlemen are not going to let you
die," reckoned rescue long about the time
my arms gave out. The furnace, meant for
nippy fall and spring, is not keeping up;
the thermostat reads 45 degrees.
This is not wonderful, but it's not serious.
I begin dripping the faucets.
I am ready.

What's serious are these swaddled windowpanes,
room after room, snow-crusted to the roof line,
encasing me in an aquarium where light
enters stripped of color while wind
plays the chimneys like jugs of moonshine;
the ship's model positioned in the bay window
in a plexiglass case holding course
at the bottom of a sea of ice; the minimal

verbs "to be" and "to have";
the day ahead unexplored and limited
as a blank piece of paper;
this prison;
this absolute freedom.

The Promised Land

When my poems are published, there they are,
out there, on slick paper, on newstands, people's
coffee tables, and they look like
they have my genes. That's
my bony butt, my spineless face!
I could die. They need
correction, those no-good, lousy, dirty-rotten,
good-for-nothings, think they're such big shots,
that disgusting, nauseating load,
and they're like dead things. They have
no connection with me. They need to be
wiped off the face of the earth. And I get it, finally, how
my mother and father could look at
four blond, blue-eyed children
and want to murder them, how, seeing only good
residing in oneself, it is possible to look at
what one gives birth to and see only
the other half of one's soul made flesh, how
that unhoused, dispossessed claim
screeches and whirs through the air frantic for lodging, how
children, soft-boned, hungry and roomy, understand
and take in the unwanted, how it is that
when I see my poems in print, my
distressingly blue-eyed blond poems,
I want to pick them up between thumb and forefinger and,
holding them far out from the body, walk them down to the
   water

and drown them, the way, the way, the
way my brother Dallas, having survived cancer—after being
diagnosed hopeless—a sign
that he was, our parents said,
favored by God, and thinking
he'd escaped our parents, too, having made
a place for himself in a city apart,
took himself, the day the moving vans
deposited his parents' possessions—three months after he was
diagnosed cured—in the outskirts of the city he'd escaped to,
out to their new house, and
seeing the cane-bottomed chairs, the Hepplewhite table,
the Virginia cupboard with the missing pane, the spool beds,
the robin's egg blue camel-back sofa, all the memories emerge
one by one from the van, seeing
that it was true, that they were come,
picked himself up by the scruff of the neck,
went back to his bachelor pad, put Erich Maria Remarque's
Heaven Has No Favorites—look, he was only 22—
on his bedside table, and,
holding himself far out from the body,
got into his red MG TC, drove to the quarry at White, Ga., and
drowned Dallas.

Grandmother's Rug

32" × 43" rug of useful size, hooked c. 1911 by mountain women
according to a design by the artist Mary Evelyn Kirk. First phase Cubism
of significant original vision. Last completed work. $750.00
—INSURANCE APPRAISAL

On days I'm not listening,
when the words escape rebellious as steam
from the snap-bean pot, hustle, answering
only to me, into lines and stanzas,
I kneel on Grandmother's rug come to rest
on a herringbone floor four flights over Manhattan,
and cup my hand around the precise green lobe,
the blood rim of an ear full of yarn sky
floating detached in a divided eternity since 1911—
two years before the Armory Show—and I whisper
into the hooked earth of Virginia, "Hey, Grandmom,
by heavens, I'm doing it." She was so good

in 1912 she came home, Mary Evelyn Kirk,
married Mr. Hammond, who, ever after, called her
Miz Hammond, even in her dreams, she,
who bore him five live children, went to the dances
and Hot Springs, wore blue lace and gardenias,
and never painted again. And yet the artist

traded poems with me like secrets—sonnets, couplets,
villanelles tucked in with birthday checks, saying
hers were not so good—and filled the ballroom attic
with flower containers, collecting hundreds, thousands,
from all the accessible countries, England to China,
in all formalities, earthenware to Lalique,
leaping centuries, Etruscan to Steuben,

mustering them on long rows of tables
like an army of women, their throats and mouths
open in a howl to the eaves. Every morning

she tied a straw hat under her chin,
slipped an ancient egg basket on her arm,
and browsed in the gardens, selecting her palette:
roses and moonwort, dahlias and peonies,
snippets of ivy, boxwood, sorghum—even
kale and eggplant had beauty. Then
she'd climb to the attic, walk up and down
between the tables, studying the containers,
choosing which mouths to give voice to. By eleven,
still lifes supported by frogs and chicken wire,
hidden inside Delft and Limoges and Gallé,
posed on flat lacquer stands in all the rooms,
or waited in a line by the front door for judging,
a few so good, to me they're committed
as oil to canvas, as Manet's *Pinks and Clematis,*
Van Gogh's *Oleanders,* the rest
captured in a steamer trunk of Blue Ribbons,
the way the meadow and the garden
reside in potpourri. Even so, the unused

cerulean blues, the cadmium yellows
entered her bones, crippling her with nagging,
complaints, hypochondria, real arthritis dwarfing her

like the bonsai trees of her Late Period
she sculpted, pruning the roots, pinching
back and wiring shoots and branches until
they were pictures of the wind. So

on the best days, when my ear is full of sky
and the words come so good it feels like 1911
must have felt to her, I like to give her a tickle.
I dance barefoot on her rug, planting red,
harlot toenails first in the scarlet, bourrée,
bourrée into the beige, lopsided earth, holding
on demi-point in the eye that looks like an egg
sunnyside up and fertilized, a couple of tendus
over the ear in the windowpane dividing eternity,
and in the field where color and line connect
two feet off the frontal plane, the mirage
enters my legs, travels into my hips and trunk,
keeping my bones straight and supple, and I sing
loud enough for Roanoke.